CUL DE SAC
(BUM OF BAG)
Guide du français courant
(Guide to the running French)

————————Jean-Loup Chiflet————————

CUL DE SAC
(BUM OF BAG)
Guide du français courant
(Guide to the running French)

Illustrated by
CLAB

ANGUS
& ROBERTSON
PUBLISHERS

ANGUS & ROBERTSON PUBLISHERS

Unit 4, Eden Park, 31 Waterloo Road,
North Ryde, NSW, Australia 2113, and
16 Golden Square, London W1R 4BN,
United Kingdom

First published in France, as
Sky my husband! Ciel mon mari!,
by Éditions Hermé in 1985
This English-language edition
first published in Australia
by Angus & Robertson Publishers
and in the United Kingdom by
Angus & Robertson (UK) in 1987

Copyright © Éditions Hermé, October 1985
Copyright © Angus & Robertson 1987, English-language edition

National Library of Australia
Cataloguing-in-publication data.

Chiflet, Jean-Loup.
  Cul de sac.

  ISBN 0 207 15339 6.

  1. French language — Glossaries, vocabularies, etc. —
  English — Anecdotes, facetiae, satire, etc. I. Clab.
  II. Title. III. Title: Bum of bag.
448'.3'421

Typeset in Hong Kong by Graphicraft Typesetters Ltd
Printed in the United Kingdom

PREFACE

Throughout history France has regularly found herself at the mercy of invading enemies. The aim of the invader was usually to wrest French territory from its rightful owners but in the 1950s a more insidious fifth column slipped ashore, its mission to undermine the French language itself.

Once again France found herself under the conqueror's heel or, more precisely, under his bowler hat. Hordes of *franglais* speakers swarmed off Channel ferries, invading the sacred soil of France and destroying all before them *comme des bulldozers*, ravaging *les sex-shops*, transfixing *coq au vin* on the spits *de leurs barbecues* and ordering *des hot dogs* from traditional French cafés (soon to be transformed *en drugstores*).

The average Frog-in-the-street couldn't believe his ears. While he may have accepted *le chewing-gum*, courtesy of the liberating GIs who danced *le be-bop* on *le week-end* in *les dancings*, this latest assault on his language was just too much to bear. France had not been so insulted by "perfidious Albion" since the days of Joan of Arc and Napoleon.

Enough was enough! The French Government itself intervened and in 1977 introduced a law which forbade the use of English words in official communications. *Le bulldozer* became *le bouteur*, *l'interview* gave way to *l'entretien* and *le container* modified its vowels to become *le conteneur*.

Too little too late, alas. "Franglicisms" had reached the point of no return and no-one could tell the average Frenchman not to *faire le jogging* around *le parking*. Even Monsieur Robert (of dictionary fame) blithely defined "*une personne sexy*" as "*ayant du sex-appeal*". The last bastion had fallen. Today Robert, tomorrow France!

But brave France had fought worse battles than this. A subtle countermeasure was devised to stop the rot, or at least to slow it in its tracks. As the (French) saying goes: "If you're short on oil and vocabulary, make up for it in ideas and humour." Given that English words have become entrenched in the French language, why not subject them to the influence of Gallic cuisine — and serve them up on a silver platter for comparison with the elegance, subtlety, economy and piquancy of the French ingredients. Try this recipe:

Take a normal French word, in the literal or figurative sense of that word, depending on the season and the available ingredients.

Establish the literal meaning. If there are several, choose one at random.

Insert the word in an expression (proverb, quotation, officialese, everyday speech, etc.). Should you be fond of spicy food, don't hesitate to add a pinch of slang.

Translate the expression word-for-word.

Serve.

The author has personally spent the past few years in the depths of his laboratory patiently formulating and testing the recipes of this most unique of *nouvelles cuisines*. An especially succulent item serves as the book's title.

But softly softly catchy monkey (as the curious English say). Do not dive at lost body (*plonger à corps perdu*) into this fabulous guide to modern French — you will be better served if you nibble on a few choice items at each sitting. In this way you will soon learn to savour the natural superiority of the French dish.

This guide is designed to be read from left to right and from A to Z. The arrangement of entries can be seen clearly from the example on the page opposite.

As your linguistic apprenticeship proceeds, you will be able to check your progress using the revision exercises strategically placed throughout the book.

À la bonne votre! (At the good yours!)

Jean-Loup Chiflet   *John-Wolf Whistle*

HOW THIS GUIDE WORKS

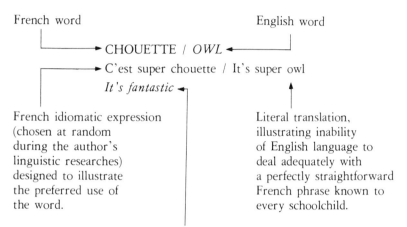

French word   English word

CHOUETTE / *OWL*

C'est super chouette / It's super owl

It's fantastic

French idiomatic expression   Literal translation,
(chosen at random   illustrating inability
during the author's   of English language to
linguistic researches)   deal adequately with
designed to illustrate   a perfectly straightforward
the preferred use of   French phrase known to
the word.   every schoolchild.

Idiomatic (and even correct) translation
given by the dictionary. Used in
examinations and in Anglosaxon milieux.

LESSON 1

Aa

ABOIS / *BARKS*
Être aux abois / To be at the barks
To have your back to the wall

AFFICHE / *POSTER*
Tenir l'affiche / To hold the poster
To have a long run (film, play etc.)

1

ALLER / *TO GO*

Ça ira, ça ira! / It will go, it will go
French revolutionary slogan

ÂNE / *DONKEY*

Passer du coq à l'âne / To pass from cock to donkey
To change the subject

ANGLAIS / *ENGLISH*

Filer à l'anglaise / To spin at the English
To take French leave

APPAREIL / *CAMERA*
Dans le plus simple appareil / In the plainest camera
In your birthday suit

ARRACHER / *TO PULL OUT*
Travailler d'arrache-pied / To work of pull out foot
To work like a navvy

ASSIETTE / *PLATE*
Ne pas être dans son assiette / Not to be in one's plate
To be out of sorts

AUBERGE / *INN*
Nous ne sommes pas sortis de l'auberge / We are not out of the inn
We're not out of the woods yet

LESSON 2

Bb

BAC / *FERRY*
Passer son bac / To pass one's ferry
To graduate

BAIN / *BATH*
Au bain-marie / At the bath-Mary
In the double-boiler

BAISER / *TO KISS*
Il s'est fait vachement baisé / He has been cowly kissed
He's really been had

BALAI / *BROOM*
Il a cinquante balais / He has fifty brooms
He is fifty

BALANCER / *TO BALANCE*
Je m'en contre-balance / I am counter-balancing of it
I don't give a damn
Balancer une vanne / To balance a sluice
To take a dig (at someone)
Être bien balancée / To be well balanced
To have a good figure

BALEINE / *WHALE*
Une baleine de parapluie / A whale of umbrella
An umbrella spoke

BANDE / *GANG*
Écouter une bande / To hear a gang
To listen to a tape

BARBE / *BEARD*
Être barbant / To be bearding
To be boring
La barbe! / The beard!
What a bore!
Au nez et à la barbe de quelqu'un / At the nose and at the beard of
somebody
Right under one's nose

BATEAU / *BOAT*
Il m'a monté un bateau / He climbed me up a boat
He led me up the garden path

BÂTIMENT / *BUILDING*
Quand le bâtiment va, tout va! / When the building goes, everything
goes!
French idiom which means that the economy is going well

BAVER / *TO SLAVER*

En baver des ronds de chapeau / To slaver rounds of hat
To have your eyes popping out of your head

BEC / *BEAK*

Tomber sur un bec / To fall on a beak
To come up against a snag
Clouer le bec / To nail the beak
To shut (someone) up

BÊCHER / *TO DIG*

Un bêcheur / A digger
A toffee-nose

BERGÈRE / *SHEPHERDESS*

Les Folies Bergère / The Shepherdess Madnesses
Very famous French cabaret

BESOIN / *NEED*

Faire ses besoins / To do one's needs
To spend a penny

BÊTE / *BEAST*

Chercher la petite bête / To look for the little beast
To nit-pick

BEURRE / *BUTTER*

Être beurré / To be buttered
To be pickled

BIDE (colloquial) / *STOMACH*
Faire un bide / To make a stomach
To have egg on your face

BIDON / *JERRY CAN*
C'est bidon / It is jerry can
It's baloney
Se bidonner / To jerry-can oneself
To fall about laughing

BLANC / *WHITE*
Faire chou blanc / To make white cabbage
To fail completely

BLEU / *BLUE*
N'y voir que du bleu / To see only blue
Not to smell a rat

BŒUF / *BEEF*
Un effet bœuf / A beef effect
An impressive effect

BOMBE / *BOMB*
Aller faire la bombe / To go and make the bomb
To paint the town red

BON / *GOOD*
Bon sang de bonsoir / Good blood of good evening
Damn and blast!

BOND / *JUMP*
Faire faux bond / To make wrong jump
To stand (someone) up

BONHOMME / *GENTLEMAN*
Aller son petit bonhomme de chemin / To go one's little gentleman of
path
To go one's own sweet way

BOUCHER / *TO CORK*
En boucher un coin / To cork a corner
To take the wind out of someone's sails

BOUQUET / *BUNCH*
C'est le bouquet! / It is the bunch!
That takes the biscuit!

BOURSE / *STOCK EXCHANGE*
La bourse ou la vie! / The stock exchange or the life!
Your money or your life!

BOUTEILLE / *BOTTLE*

Avoir de la bouteille / To have some bottle

To be long in the tooth

BRAS / *ARM*

À bras-le-corps / At arm-the-body

Around the waist

BUT / *GOAL*

De but en blanc / From goal to white

At the drop of a hat

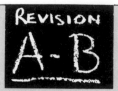

Il a filé à l'anglaise dans le plus simple appareil à notre nez et à notre barbe parce qu'il était beurré et nous cherchions la petite bête en lui balançant une vanne.

He span at the English in the plainest camera at our nose and our beard because he was buttered and we were looking for the little beast in balancing him a sluice.

ÇA / *THAT*
Il ne pense qu'à ça / He only thinks of that
He has a dirty mind

CACHET / *PILL*
Le cachet de la poste faisant foi / The pill of the mail making faith
Date as per postmark

CADAVRE / *CORPSE*
Un cadavre ambulant / A travelling corpse
Death warmed up

CAFARD / *COCKROACH*
Avoir le cafard / To have the cockroach
To be down in the dumps

CAISSE / *CRATE*
Jouer de la grosse caisse / To play big crate
To play bass drum

CANARD / *DUCK*
Faire un canard / To make a duck
To hit a wrong note

CARTE / *MAP*
Brouiller les cartes / To mix up the maps
To complicate matters

CASSER / TO BREAK

Ca ne casse pas des briques / It does not break bricks
It's nothing to write home about
Casser la croûte / To break the crust
To have a bite to eat

CATHOLIQUE / CATHOLIC

Ne pas avoir l'air catholique / Not to have the Catholic air
To look shady

CAUSER / TO SPEAK

Cause toujours, tu m'intéresses / Speak always, you are interesting me
Talk as much as you like, you don't impress me

CHAGRIN / SORROW

Diminuer comme une peau de chagrin / Diminish like a skin of sorrow
To shrink away

CHAMPIGNON / MUSHROOM

Appuyer sur le champignon / To press on the mushroom
To accelerate

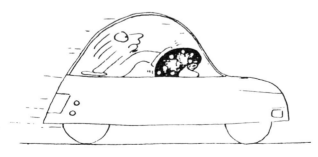

CHEVAL / *HORSE*
Ce n'est pas le mauvais cheval / He is not the bad horse
He's not a bad guy

CHEVILLE / *ANKLE*
La cheville ouvrière / The working ankle
The king pin

CHÈVRE / *GOAT*
Chèvrefeuille / Goatleaf
Honeysuckle

CHIEN / *DOG*
Avoir du chien / To have dog
To be sexy

CHOCOLAT / *CHOCOLATE*
Être chocolat / To be chocolate
To have been swindled

CHOSE / *THING*
Je me sens tout chose / I feel all thing
I feel under the weather

CHOU / *CABBAGE*
C'est son chou-chou / He is her cabbage-cabbage
He's her pet
Chou à la crème / Cabbage at the cream
Cream puff

CHOUETTE / OWL
C'est super chouette / It is super owl
It's fantastic

CINQ / FIVE
Je lui ai dit les cinq lettres / I told him the five letters
I told him where to get off

CIRER / TO POLISH
N'avoir rien à cirer / To have nothing to polish
Not to give a damn

CLIQUES / CLICKS
Prendre ses cliques et ses claques / To take one's clicks and one's
clacks
To pack up and push off

CLOCHE / BELL
Déménager à la cloche de bois / To move at the wooden bell
To do a moonlight flit

COCHON / PIG
Copains comme cochons / Friends like pigs
Inseparable friends

COIN / CORNER
Aller au petit coin / To go to the little corner
To go to the loo
Coin-coin / Corner-corner
Quack-quack

15

COMMISSION / *ERRAND*

Faire une petite commission / To make a small errand
To go for a pee

COMMODE / *CHEST OF DRAWERS*

Ce n'est pas commode / It is not chest of drawers
It's not easy

COMPTER / *TO COUNT*

Compter pour du beurre / To count for butter
To count for nothing
Son compte est bon / His account is good
He's had it

CONCERT / *CONCERT*

Aller de concert / To go of concert
To go together

16

CONTE / *STORY*
Un conte à dormir debout / A story to sleep standing up
A cock-and-bull story

CONTRAVENTION / *PARKING TICKET*
Faire sauter une contravention / To make a parking ticket jump
To get out of paying a fine

COUCHE / *BED*
Il en tient une couche / He is holding a bed of it
He's a cretin

COURANT / *CURRENT*
Tenez-moi au courant / Keep me at the current
Keep me informed

COURIR / *TO RUN*
Courir sur le haricot / To run on the bean
To get on someone's nerves

CRÊPE / *PANCAKE*
Crêper le chignon / To pancake the bun
To tear each other's hair out

CROIX / *CROSS*
Croix de bois, / Wooden cross,
croix de fer, / iron cross,
si je mens je vais en enfer / if I lie I go to hell
Cross my heart and hope to die

CUIRE / *TO COOK*

C'est du tout cuit / It is all cooked
It's in the bag
Être dur à cuire / To be hard to cook
To put up strong resistance
Les carottes sont cuites / The carrots are cooked
The die is cast

CUL / *BUM*

Cul de sac / Bum of bag
Cul de sac
Bouche en cul de poule / Mouth in bum of chicken
Pursed lips
Faire cul sec / To make dry bum
To down (a drink) in one
Être comme cul et chemise / To be like bum and shirt
To be the best of friends

Tirer au cul / To pull at the bum
To malinger
En avoir plein le cul / To have the bum full of it
To be fed up
La peau du cul / The skin of the bum
Very expensive

Parce qu'il ne pensait qu'à ça, il prit ses cliques et ses claques pour déménager à la cloche de bois pour une super fille chouette qui avait du chien. Il devint son chou-chou et ils sont maintenant comme cul et chemise.

Because he was only thinking of that, he took his clicks and his clacks to move at the wooden bell to a super owl girl who had dog. He became her cabbage-cabbage and they are now like bum and shirt.

DÉFAUT / *DEFECT*

Faire défaut / To make defect
To lack

DEMAIN / *TOMORROW*

Ce n'est pas demain la veille / It is not tomorrow the day before
Don't hold your breath waiting

DÉMASQUER / *TO UNCOVER*

Il a démasqué ses batteries / He uncovered his batteries
He laid his cards on the table

DENT / *TOOTH*

Avoir une dent contre quelqu'un / To have a tooth opposite somebody
To have a grudge against somebody

DEVANT / *IN FRONT*

Gros Jean comme devant / Big John like in front
Like a twit

DIEU / *GOD*

Vingt dieux, la belle église! / Twenty gods, the nice church!
Good heavens above!

DIRE / *TO SAY*

Le qu'en-dira-t-on / The what-will-one-say of it
What will the neighbours say

DRAP / *BED SHEET*

Être dans de beaux draps / To be in nice bed sheets

To be in a fix

EMPRUNTER / *TO BORROW*
Avoir un air emprunté / To have a borrowed air
To look uncomfortable
Emprunter une route / To borrow a road
To take a certain route

ENLEVER / *TO REMOVE*
Il l'a enlevé de haute lutte / He removed it with high struggle
He won it fair and square

ENTENDRE / *TO HEAR*
À bon entendeur, salut! / At good hearer, goodbye!
A word to the wise is enough

ÉPINGLE / *PIN*

Tiré à quatre épingles / Pulled at four pins

Dressed up like a dog's dinner

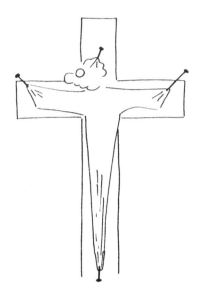

24

FACTURE / *INVOICE*

Être de bonne facture / To be of good invoice
To be of good quality

FAIRE / *TO MAKE*

Être fait comme un rat / To be made like a rat
To be cornered
Faire le beau / To do the nice
To beg

FER / *IRON*

Un chemin de fer / A path of iron
A railway

FESSE / *BUTTOCK*
Un fesse-Mathieu / A buttock-Matthew
A skinflint

FEUILLE / *LEAF*
Dur de la feuille / Hard of the leaf
Hard of hearing

FIER / *PROUD*
Fier-à-bras / Proud-to-arm
A wise guy

FIL / *THREAD*
Aller au fil de l'eau / To go at the thread of water
To go with the flow
Passer au fil de l'épée / To pass at the thread of the sword
To run (someone) through with a sword

Fils de la vierge / Threads of the virgin
Gossamer
Un coupe de fil / A knock of the thread
A phone call

FINIR / *TO END*
Finir en beauté / To end in beauty
To finish brilliantly

FLEUR / *FLOWER*
Elle est trop fleur bleue / She is too blue flower
She's too sentimental
Un chou-fleur / A cabbage-flower
A cauliflower

FOIE / *LIVER*
Avoir les foies / To have the livers
To be scared stiff

FOND / *BOTTOM*

Aller à fond de train / To go at bottom of train

To go flat out

FOURRER / *TO STICK, SHOVE*

Tu t'es fourré le doigt dans le nez / You have stuck your finger in your nose

You haven't a clue, have you?

FRAIS / *EXPENSES*

Me voilà frais / I am expenses

I'm in a pretty mess

FRAISE / *STRAWBERRY*

Sucrer les fraises / To sugar the strawberries

To be old and doddery

Ramener sa fraise / To bring back one's strawberry

To shove one's oar in

FRANC / *FRANK*
Franc du collier / Frank of the collar
Hard-working

FRAPPER / *TO HIT*
Ne vous frappez pas / Don't hit yourself
Don't get excited

FROID / *COLD*
Un froid de canard / A cold of duck
Brass-monkey weather

GAGNER / *TO WIN*
Un gagne-pain / A win-bread
Just a job

GAILLARD / *FINE FELLOW*
Le gaillard d'arrière / The fine fellow behind
The quarter-deck

GARDER / *TO KEEP*
Garde-à-vous! / Keep to you!
Attention!
Garder un chien de sa chienne / To keep a dog from one's bitch
To have it in for someone

GARE / *STATION*
Sans crier gare / Without shouting station
Without warning

GAUCHE / *LEFT*
Passer l'arme à gauche / To pass the weapon to the left
To kick the bucket

GONFLER / *TO INFLATE*
Il est vachement gonflé / He is cowly inflated
He's got a cheek

GORGE / *THROAT*
Faire des gorges chaudes / To make warm throats
To pour scorn

GROS / *BIG*
Gros temps / Big weather
Stormy weather
Ma grosse choucroute / My big sauerkraut
My sweetie-pie

GUÊPE / WASP
Pas folle la guêpe! / Not crazy the wasp!
Not born yesterday

GUERRE / WAR
C'est de bonne guerre / It is of good war
Fair's fair

Il a les foies parce qu'il est fait comme un rat. Il a démasqué ses batteries et rendu le chou-fleur volé au marché.

He has the livers because he is made like a rat. He has uncovered his batteries and returned the cabbage-flower stolen in the market.

LESSON 8

HI

HALEINE / *BREATH*

De longue haleine / Of long breath
Long term

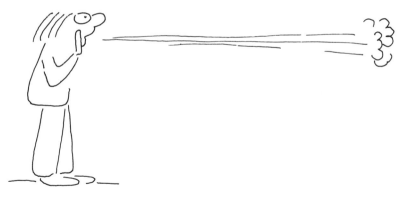

HANNETON / *BEETLE*

Pas piqué des hannetons! / Not picked of the beetles!
A helluva...

HARICOTS / *BEANS*
La fin des haricots / The end of the beans
The last straw

HAUT / *HIGH*
Tenir le haut du pavé / To hold the high of the pavement
To lord it

HEURE / *HOUR*
À la bonne heure! / At the good hour!
Well done!

HUILE / *OIL*

Ça baigne dans l'huile / It is bathing in the oil
Everything's going smoothly

INCENDIER / *TO BURN DOWN*

Je me suis fait incendier / I made myself burn down
I've been caught

JAMBE / *LEG*

Ça me fait une belle jambe / It makes me a nice leg
That won't get me very far
Faire des ronds de jambe / To make rounds of leg
To bow and scrape

JAUNE / *YELLOW*

Rire jaune / To laugh yellow
To give a forced laugh

JEU / *GAME*

Un jeu d'écritures / A game of writings
A dummy entry
Être vieux jeu / To be old game
To be old-fashioned

JONC / *REED*
Tu me pèles le jonc! / You are peeling my reed!
You get up my nose!

JOUER / *TO PLAY*
Jouer son va-tout / To play one's go all
To play one's last card

KIF / *MARIJUANA*
Kif-kif bourricot / Marijuana-marijuana donkey
It's all the same

LÀ / *HERE*

Une Marie-couche-toi-là / A Mary-lie-down-here

A tart

LAMPE / *LAMP*

S'en mettre plein la lampe / To fill full one's lamp

To stuff one's face

LANGUE / *TONGUE*
Donner sa langue au chat / To give one's tongue to the cat
To give up
Avoir une langue bien pendue / To have a well-hung tongue
To be a chatter box
Prendre langue / To take tongue
To make contact

LARGE / *WIDE*
Ne pas en mener large / Not to lead wide of it
To be scared

LÉGUME / *VEGETABLE*
Une grosse légume / A big vegetable
A V.I.P.

LETTRE / *LETTER*
Au pied de la lettre / At the foot of the letter
Literally
Avoir des lettres / To have letters
To be cultured

LIEU / *PLACE*
J'ai tout lieu de croire / I have all place to believe
Everything leads me to believe

LIÈVRE / *HARE*
Soulever un lièvre / To lift up a hare
To stir up a hornet's nest

39

LIGNE / *LINE*

Entrer en ligne de compte / To enter in line of count
To enter into consideration

LOURD / *HEAVY*

Il n'en sait pas lourd / He does not know heavy of it
He doesn't know much about it

J'ai tout lieu de croire que c'est une grosse légume qui a une langue bien pendue et qui tient le haut du pavé en s'en mettant plein la lampe.

I have all place to believe that he is a big vegetable who has a well-hung tongue and who holds the high of the pavement in filling full his lamp.

LESSON 11

Mm

MÂCHER / *TO CHEW*

Ne pas mâcher ses mots / Not to chew one's words
Not to mince words

MAILLE / *STITCH*

Avoir maille à partir / To have stitch to leave
To have a bone to pick

MAIN / HAND

Gagner haut la main / To win high the hand
To win hands down
En venir aux mains / To come to the hands of it
To come to blows
Avoir la main malheureuse / To have the unhappy hand
To be clumsy
Passer la main dans le dos / To pass the hand in the back
To flatter

MAISON / HOUSE

C'est gros comme une maison / It is big like a house
It's as plain as the nose on your face

MAÎTRE / MASTER

Pour un coup d'essai, / For a blow of try,
c'est un coup de maître / it is a blow of master
It's a very good first attempt

MAL / BAD

Avoir le mal du pays / To have the bad of the country
To be homesick
Être mal en point / To be bad in point
To be poorly
Se trouver mal / To find oneself bad
To faint
Tomber mal / To fall bad
To come at the wrong moment

MALHEUR / BAD LUCK

Faire un malheur / To do a bad luck
To be very successful

MANCHE / *HANDLE*

Ne jetez pas le manche après la cognée / Don't throw the handle after the axe

Don't throw the baby out with the bathwater

Conduire comme un manche / To drive like a handle

To be a rotten driver

MANGER / *TO EAT*

Manger du curé / To eat priest

To be a priest hater

Manger le morceau / To eat the bite

To spill the beans

MARCHER / *TO WALK*

Faire marcher à la baguette / To make walk at the stick

To rule with a rod of iron

MARI / *HUSBAND*

Ciel, mon mari! / Sky, my husband!

My god! My husband!

MARRON / *BROWN*

Un avocat marron / A brown avocado

A shady lawyer

MARTEAU / *HAMMER*

Être marteau / To be hammer

To be crazy

MEILLEUR / *BEST*

J'en passe, et des meilleures! / I am passing some and of the best!

And that's not all!

43

MÊME / SAME

Être à même de / To be at the same of
To be able to
C'est du pareil au même / It is of the same to the same
It's six of one, half a dozen of the other

MER / SEA

Ce n'est pas la mer à boire / It is not the sea to drink
It's not that difficult

MERCI / THANK YOU

À merci / At thank you
At pleasure

MONDE / WORLD

Il y a du monde au balcon / There is some world at the balcony
She's big busted

MONSIEUR / GENTLEMAN

Un croque-monsieur / A bite-gentleman
A toasted ham and cheese sandwich

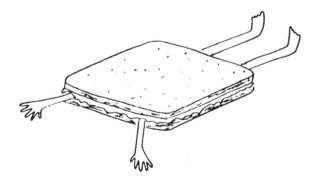

MONTER / *TO GO UP*
Monter en épingle / To go up in safety pin
To blow out of all proportion

MORT / *DEATH*
À l'article de la mort / At the article of the death
At the point of death

MOT / *WORD*
Le grand mot est lâché / The big word is loosened
The cat's out of the bag
Ne pas dire un traître mot / Not to say a traitor word
Not to breathe a single word

MOUCHE / *FLY*
Prendre la mouche / To take the fly
To get huffy
Faire mouche / To do fly
To hit the bull's eye
Être une fine mouche / To be a fine fly
To be a sly minx

MOURIR / *TO DIE*
Mourir à petit feu / To die at little fire
To fade away

MUR / *WALL*
Raser les murs / To shave the walls
To keep a low profile

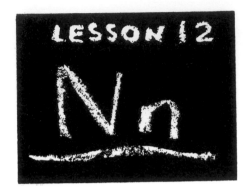

LESSON 12

Nn

NEZ / *NOSE*

Faire un pied de nez / To make a foot of nose

To thumb one's nose

NŒUD / KNOT
À la mords-moi le nœud / At the bite-me the knot
Dodgy
Un sac de nœuds / A bag of knots
A can of worms

NOIR / BLACK
Broyer du noir / To crush black
To be depressed

NOM / NAME
Un nom à coucher dehors / A name to sleep outside
An unpronounceable name

WILLIAM LLANTISILIOGOGOCH

REVISION
M-N

J'avais maille à partir avec un avocat marron à la mords-moi le nœud au nom à coucher dehors et qui avait pris la mouche et ne mâchait pas ses mots.

I had stitch to leave with a brown avocado at the bite-me the knot who has a name to sleep outside and who had taken the fly and was not chewing his words.

ODEUR / *SMELL*

En odeur de sainteté / In smell of holiness

In somebody's good graces

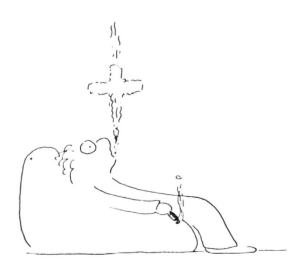

ŒIL / *EYE*

Avoir le coup d'œil / To have the blow of eye
To have a good eye
Œil de bœuf / Eye of beef
A round dormer window
Je m'en bats l'œil / I beat my eye
I don't care a hoot
Coûter les yeux de la tête / To cost the eyes of the head
To be very expensive

ŒUF / *EGG*

Faire d'un œuf un bœuf / To make an ox from an egg
To make a mountain out of a molehill

OREILLE / *EAR*

Avoir la puce à l'oreille / To have the flea at the ear
To be suspicious

ORIGINE / *ORIGIN*
Rejoindre son corps d'origine / To rejoin one's origin's body
To rejoin one's regiment

OS / *BONE*
Tomber sur un os / To fall down on a bone
To hit a problem

OUI / *YES*
Un béni oui-oui / A blessed yes-yes
A yes-man

PAIN / *BREAD*

Ça ne mange pas de pain / It doesn't eat bread

It's not important

PAPIER / *PAPER*

Être dans les petits papiers de quelqu'un / To be in the little papers of
somebody

To be in somebody's good books

PAQUET / *PACKAGE*

Mettre le paquet / To put the package
To pull out all stops

PARFUM / *PERFUME*

Être au parfum / To be at the perfume
To be in the know

PARLER / *TO SPEAK*

Parler à bâtons rompus / To speak at broken sticks
To jump from subject to subject
Tu parles Charles! / You speak Charles!
You don't say!

PASSER / *TO PASS*

Passer sur le billard / To pass on the billiard-table
To have an operation
Passer à la casserole / To pass at the saucepan
To kill or *to screw*
Maison de passe / House of pass
Brothel

PÊCHE / *PEACH*

Je n'ai pas la pêche / I do not have the peach
I'm a bit down

PÉDALER / *TO PEDAL*

Pédaler dans la choucroute / To pedal in the sauerkraut
To get nowhere fast

PEINTURE / *PAINTING*

Elle ne peut pas le voir en peinture / She cannot see him in painting
She can't stand the sight of him

PELLICULE / *FILM*

Avoir des pellicules / To have films
To have dandruff

PENSER / TO THINK
Un pense-bête / A think-beast
A reminder

PERDRE / TO LOSE
Perdre la boule / To lose the ball
To go crazy

PÈRE / FATHER
Allez donc, ce n'est pas mon père! / Go then, he is not my father!
I don't care!

PETIT / LITTLE
Au petit bonheur, la chance / At the little luck, the chance
At random

PIÈCE / COIN
Être tout d'une pièce / To be all of a coin
To be blunt

PIED / *FOOT*

Marcher à cloche-pied / To walk at bell-foot
To hop
Elle chante comme un pied / She sings like a foot
She's a lousy singer
Ne me casse pas les pieds / Don't break my feet
Please leave me alone
Prendre son pied / To take one's foot
To get a kick out of something

PILE / *BATTERY*

Tomber pile / To fall battery
To happen just at the right moment

PIPE / *PIPE*

Nom d'une pipe! / Name of a pipe!
My god!

PLAISIR / *PLEASURE*

Au plaisir, ces messieurs-dames! / At the pleasure, these gentlemen-
                                    ladies!
See you later!

PLANCHER / *FLOOR*

Le plancher des vaches / The floor of the cows
Dry land

PLANTER / *TO PLANT*

Se planter / To plant oneself
To fail
Aller planter ses choux / To go and plant cabbages
To retire to the country

PLAT / *FLAT*

Tomber à plat / To fall at flat
To miss the boat
Être à plat / To be at flat
To be washed out
Faire du plat à quelqu'un / To make flat to someone
To chat (someone) up
Battre à plate couture / To beat at flat seam
To beat (someone) hollow

PLEIN / *FULL*

En mettre plein la vue / To put full the sight of it
To dazzle someone

PLIER / *TO FOLD*

Plier bagage / To fold luggage
To pack up and leave

POIL / *HAIR*

Être à poil / To be at hair
To be naked
Reprendre du poil de la bête / To take back the hair from the beast
To become one's own self again

POIREAU / *LEEK*

Faire le poireau / To make the leek
To cool one's heels

POMPE / *PUMP*

Aller à toute pompe / To go at all pump
To go flat out
Être en dehors de ses pompes / To be out of one's pumps
To be absent-minded

PORTRAIT / *PICTURE*

Un portrait tout craché / A picture all spat
The spitting image

POSER / *TO PUT DOWN*
Poser un lapin / To put down a rabbit
To stand (someone) up

POSITION / *POSITION*
Prendre position / To take position
To take a stand
Réviser ses positions / To revise one's positions
To revise one's views

POT / *POT*
Raccommoder les pots cassés / To mend the broken pots
To get to the bottom of something
Pot-de-vin / Pot of wine
A backhander
À la fortune du pot / At the fortune of the pot
Taking pot luck
Avoir du pot / To have pot
To be lucky

POUCE / *THUMB*
Pouce! / Thumb!
Pax!

POULE / *CHICKEN*
Pied-de-poule / Foot of chicken
Hound's-tooth check
Une poule mouillée / A wet chicken
A coward
Une poule de luxe / A luxurious chicken
A high-class call girl
Chair de poule / Flesh of chicken
Gooseflesh

POUSSER / *TO PUSH*
À la va-comme-je-te-pousse / At the go like I push you
Any which way

PRISE / *GRIP*
Une prise de bec / A grip of beak
An argument
Prise de son / Grip of sound
Sound recording

PROPRE / *CLEAN*
C'est du propre! / It is clean!
What a shambles!
Un propre à rien / A clean to nothing
A good-for-nothing

LESSON 15

QUART / *QUARTER*
Au quart de tour / At the quarter of turn
Immediately

QUATORZE / *FOURTEEN*
C'est parti comme en quatorze / It is gone like in fourteen
It's started well

QUATRE / *FOUR*
Se mettre en quatre / To put oneself in four
To bend over backwards

QUELQU'UN / *SOMEBODY*

Avoir quelqu'un à la bonne / To have somebody at the good
To be fond of somebody

Je n'ai pas la pêche car je vais passer sur le billiard. J'ai la chair de poule car cela me coûtera les yeux de la tête et après je serai obligé de marcher à cloche-pied.

I don't have the peach because I am going to pass on the billiard-table. I have the flesh of chicken because it will cost me the eyes of the head and I will be obliged after to walk at bell-foot.

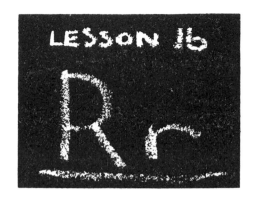

LESSON 16

Rr

RAISIN / *GRAPE*

Mi-figure, mi-raisin / Half-fig, half-grape

Neither fish nor fowl

RAT / *RAT*

Un rat d'hôtel / A hotel rat
A hotel thief
À bon chat, bon rat / At good cat, good rat
I have got your number
Un rat de bibliothèque / A library rat
A bookworm
Un rat de cave / A cellar rat
An exciseman

RAYER / *TO SCRATCH*

Un complet rayé / A scratched complete
A pin-striped suit
Être rayé des cadres / To be scratched from the frames
To be dismissed

RAYON / *RAY*

En connaître un rayon / To know one ray of it
To know a lot about it

RÉCHAUFFER / *TO REHEAT*
Réchauffer un serpent dans son sein / To reheat a snake in his breast
To nurture a viper in one's bosom

REGARD / *LOOK*
Couler un regard / To flow a look
To cast a glance

REGARDER / *TO LOOK*
Il n'est pas regardant / He is not looking
He is free with his money

RÉGIME / *DIET*
Un régime de bananes / A banana diet
A bunch of bananas

REIN / *KIDNEY*
Un tour de reins / A turn of kidneys
A sudden back pain

RENVOI / *DISMISSAL*
Faire un renvoi / To make a dismissal
To belch

RÉPONSE / *REPLY*
C'est la réponse du berger à la bergère / It is the reply of the
                                                 shepherd to the shepherdess
It's tit for tat

REVENIR / *TO COME BACK*
Un prix de revient / A price of come back
Cost price

RHUME / *COLD*
Un rhume carabiné / A rifled cold
A bad cold

ROMAINE / *COS LETTUCE*
Bon comme la romaine / Good like the cos lettuce
Done for

ROND / *ROUND*
Rond comme une queue de pelle / Round like a tail of shovel
Very drunk
Je n'ai plus un rond / I no longer have a round
I'm broke

RONGER / *TO GNAW*
Ronger son frein / To gnaw one's brake
To champ at the bit

ROUE / *WHEEL*

Sur les chapeaux de roue / On the hats of wheel
Very fast

RUE / *STREET*

Ça ne court pas les rues / It doesn't run the streets
Few and far between

LESSON 17

Ss

SAC / *BAG*
Mettre à sac / To put to bag
To rifle

SALUT / *HELLO*
Une planche de salut / A board of hello
A lifeline

SAVON / *SOAP*

Passer un savon / To pass a soap
To give (someone) a dressing-down

SECOUER / *TO SHAKE*

Secoue tes puces! / Shake your fleas!
Snap out of it

SENS / *SENSE*

Sens giratoire / Gyrating sense
Roundabout
Sens interdit / Forbidden sense
No entry

SERRER / *TO GRIP*

Serrer les fesses / To grip the buttocks
To be scared stiff

SIFFLET / *WHISTLE*

Il m'a coupé le sifflet / He cut my whistle
He left me speechless

SIX / *SIX*
À la six quatre deux / At the six four two
Any old how

SŒUR / *SISTER*
Et ta sœur? / And your sister?
Mind your own business

SONNER / *TO RING*
Être sonné / To be rung
To be knocked out

SORTIE / *WAY OUT*
Faire une sortie à quelqu'un / To make a way out to somebody
To bawl somebody out

SOUCI / *WORRY*
C'est le cadet de mes soucis / It is the junior of my worries
That's the least of my problems

SOURIS / *MOUSE*
Une chauve-souris / A bald mouse
A bat

SUISSE / *SWISS*

Un petit-suisse / A little Swiss
A soft cream cheese

Je lui ai passé un savon et je lui ai fait une sortie car comme il
était rond comme une queue de pelle, il a attrapé un tour de
reins en portant un lourd régime de bananes.

I passed him a soap and I made a way out to him because as he
was round like a tail of shovel he got a turn of kidneys in
carrying a heavy diet of bananas.

TABAC / *TOBACCO*
C'est du même tabac / It is of the same tobacco
Something like that

TABLEAU / *PAINTING*
Brosser un tableau / To brush a painting
To describe
Jouer sur les deux tableaux / To play on the two paintings
To lay odds both ways

TANNER / *TO TAN*
Que tu me tannes! / That you tan me!
You drive me up the wall

TAPER / *TO HIT*
Se taper la cloche / To hit one's bell
To eat well

TAPISSERIE / *TAPESTRY*
Faire tapisserie / To make tapestry
To be a wallflower

TARTE / *PIE*
C'est pas de la tarte! / It is not pie!
It's not easy!

TARTINE / *JAM SANDWICH*

Écrire des tartines / To write jam sandwiches

To write a lot

TEMPS / *TIME*

Un temps de chien / A time of dog

Lousy weather

TENIR / *TO HOLD*

Un tiens vaut mieux que deux tu l'auras / A hold is better than two
you will have it

A bird in the hand is worth two in the bush

TÊTE / *HEAD*

Il a une sale tête / He has a dirty head

He looks a nasty piece of work

Être la tête de Turc / To be the Turkish head

To be the scapegoat

Faire tête à queue / To make head to tail

To swing right around

Tête-bêche / Head-spade

Top to bottom

TIMBRER / *TO STAMP*
Être timbré / To be stamped
To be round the bend

TIRER / *TO SHOOT*
À tire-d'aile / At shoot-wing
Swiftly

TOMBER / *TO FALL*
Il tombe à point nommé / He falls at named point
He's arrived just in time

TOUR / *TURN*
Le Tour de France / The Turn of France
The round France cycle race
Faire un tour de cochon / To make a turn of pig
To play a dirty trick
En un tour de main / On one turn of hand
In a flash
Le tour est joué / The turn is played
The trick has worked

TOURNER / *TO TURN*
Être mal tourné / To be badly turned
To be in a bad mood

TOUT / *ALL*
Un touche-à-tout / A touch-to-all
A busybody
Jouer le tout pour le tout / To play the all for the all
To risk everything
Le Tout-Paris / The All-Paris
The smart set

TRADUIRE / *TO TRANSLATE*
Traduire quelqu'un en justice / To translate somebody in Court
To prosecute

TRAIN / *TRAIN*
Se magner le train / To move one's train
To hurry up
Filer le train / To spin the train
To follow

TRANQUILLE / *QUIET*
Tranquille comme Baptiste / Quiet like Baptiste
Very quiet

TRAVAILLER / *TO WORK*
Travailler du chapeau / To work from the hat
To be crazy

TRENTE ET UN / *THIRTY-ONE*

Se mettre sur son trente et un / To put oneself on one's thirty-one
To dress to the nines

TUER / *TO KILL*

Tuer dans l'œuf / To kill in the egg
To nip in the bud

UNE / *ONE*

Il était moins une / It was less one
It was a narrow escape
Une de perdue, dix de retrouvées / One of lost, ten of found
There are plenty more fish in the sea

LESSON 19

V v

VACHE / *COW*

C'est vachement chouette / It is cowly owl

It's very nice

VAGUE / *WAVE*
Avoir du vague à l'âme / To have wave at the soul
To feel somewhat melancholic

VALISE / *SUITCASE*
Se faire la valise / To make oneself the suitcase
To pack one's bags

VASE / *MUD*
Être vaseux / To be muddy
To be washed out

VEINE / *VEIN*
Avoir une veine de pendu / To have a vein of hanged
To be very lucky

VER / *WORM*
Ne pas être piqué des vers / Not to be picked by the worms
To be first rate

VERNIS / *VARNISH*
Être verni / To be varnished
To be lucky

VERT / *GREEN*
En raconter des vertes et des pas mûres / To tell some green and some
not ripe
To tell spicy stories

VESTE / *JACKET*
Ramasser une veste / To pick up a jacket
To come a cropper

VIE / *LIFE*
Une vie de bâton de chaise / A life of stick of chair
A rollicking life

VIEUX / *OLD*
Un vieux de la vieille / An old of the old
A very old person

VITE / *QUICK*
Vite fait sur le gaz / Quick made on the gas
Very fast

VIVRE / *TO LIVE*
Être sur le qui-vive / To be on the who-lives
To be on the alert

VOIR / *TO SEE*
Un m'as-tu vu / A have you seen me
A conceited person

VOITURE / *CAR*
En voiture Simone! / In the car Simone!
Let's get on with it

VOIX / *VOICE*
Avoir voix au chapitre / To have voice to the chapter
To have a say in the matter

VOL / *FLIGHT*
Un vol-au-vent / A flight to the wind
A pastry case

VOULOIR / *TO WANT*

En veux-tu, en voilà / Do you want some, here there are some

As many as you want

VUE / *SIGHT*

À vue de nez / At sight of nose

At a rough estimate

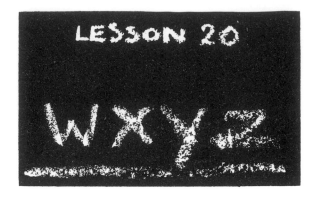

LESSON 20

WXYZ

WAGON / *WAGON*
Un wagon-lit / A wagon-bed
A sleeping car

X / *X*
Il a fait l'X / He made the X
He studied at the Polytechnic
(and is therefore one of the elite)

ZÈBRE / *ZEBRA*
Un drôle de zèbre / A funny zebra
An odd bod

ZÉRO / *ZERO*

Les avoir à zéro / To have them at zero
To be scared stiff

Je suis mal tourné car j'ai fait un tête à queue pendant le Tour de France et je les ai à zéro parce que je vais ramasser une veste.

I am badly turned because I made a head to tail during the Turn of France and I have them at zero because I am going to pick up a jacket.

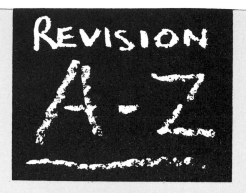

REVISION A-Z

Le béni oui-oui en venait aux mains avec une Marie-couche-toi-là qui était arrivée sans crier gare.

The blessed yes-yes was coming to the hands with a Mary-sleep-you-here who has arrived without shouting station.

Pendant que leurs maris mangeaient du curé avec leurs complets rayés, les femmes se crépaient le chignon.

While their husbands were eating priest with their scratched completes, the ladies were pancaking their buns.

Il ramena sa fraise, mi-figue mi-raisin, après avoir conduit comme un manche.

He brought back his strawberry, half-fig half-grape, after having driven like a handle.

Il a repris du poil de la bête en cassant la croûte et ça lui a coûté les yeux de la tête.

He took back the hair from the beast in breaking the crust and that cost him the eyes of the head.

Nom d'une pipe! Ce n'est pas de la tarte de faire le beau quand on a cinquante balais.

Name of a pipe! It is not pie to make the nice when one has fifty brooms.

Il a une dent contre elle parce qu'elle lui a posé un lapin.

He has a tooth opposite her because she put down a rabbit to him.

Le croque-monsieur ne baignait pas dans l'huile, alors il a demandé un petit-suisse.

The bite-gentleman was not bathing in the oil, so he asked for a little Swiss.

Elle était vachement chouette et il était tiré à quatre épingles mais avait des pellicules, alors elle refusa de passer à la casserole.

She was cowly owl and he was pulled at four pins but had films so she refused to pass at the saucepan.